WITH LOVE,

FROM: ______________________________

TO: ________________________________

DEAR ______________________________

BEST WISHES,

____

A PICTURE OF ME

Printed in Great Britain
by Amazon

44024705R00069